SHOCK ZONE™
TRUE SURVIVAL STORIES

SURVIVING
in the
WILDERNESS

BY KRISTIN MARCINIAK

Lerner Publications Company • Minneapolis

Cover image: A US Coast Guard crew helps rescue an injured man in 2011.

Lerner Publications Company
A division of Lerner Publishing Group, Inc.
241 First Avenue North
Minneapolis, MN 55401 U.S.A.

For updated reading levels and more information, look up this title
at www.lernerbooks.com.

Library of Congress Cataloging-in-Publication Data

Marciniak, Kristin.
    Surviving in the wilderness / by Kristin Marciniak.
        pages   cm. — (Shockzone—true survival stories)
    Includes index.
    ISBN 978–1–4677–1437–2 (lib. bdg. : alk. paper)
    ISBN 978–1–4677–2516–3 (eBook)
    1. Wilderness survival—Juvenile literature. I. Title.
    GV200.5.M353 2014
    613.6'9—dc23   2013022844

Manufactured in the United States of America
1—PC—12/31/13

TABLE OF CONTENTS

What started out as a fun day exploring hidden trails has **turned into a nightmare.** You're lost. A cold chill sweeps in as the sun sets. You realize you're going to have to spend the night in the woods. You're hungry and thirsty and desperate to get back home.

People get lost in the wilderness every day. Those who survive are not simply lucky. They're smart. They use their instincts and knowledge to find food, water, and shelter. They fight through nasty weather and painful injuries so they can see their loved ones once again. Every survivor's story is different. But they all have one thing in common: the will to survive.

Hike through the Amazon rain forest, climb into a rugged canyon, and trek through the lava fields of Hawaii with only your wits to help you. Would you have what it takes to survive?

One of the hardest parts of being stranded in the wilderness can be the lack of human contact.

Braving the Woods Alone

Brennan Hawkins couldn't get out of his rock climbing gear. The eleven-year-old wriggled and wiggled as he tried to loosen the ropes looped around his legs and waist. "Catch up with me!" his friend Brian called before heading down the camp road to join the other Boy Scouts for dinner.

Brennan and Brian were two of fifteen hundred Scouts spending the weekend in northeast Utah's Uinta Mountains in June 2005. Most of the Scouts on the three-day trip were fourteen or fifteen years old. Brian's dad was a Scout leader. He brought the two younger boys as his guests.

Scout rules say that you need to know where your buddy is at all times. But the sound of the dinner bell ringing in the distance reminded Brian he was hungry. He figured Brennan would untangle himself from the climbing harness and then meet him at the dinner trailer. After all, it was just a quarter of a mile (0.4 kilometers) down the road.

Instead, Brennan started walking in the opposite direction. He soon realized his mistake and turned around. But he took a wrong turn. Suddenly he did not recognize his surroundings. Brennan was lost.

The last place anyone saw Brennan was at the climbing wall.

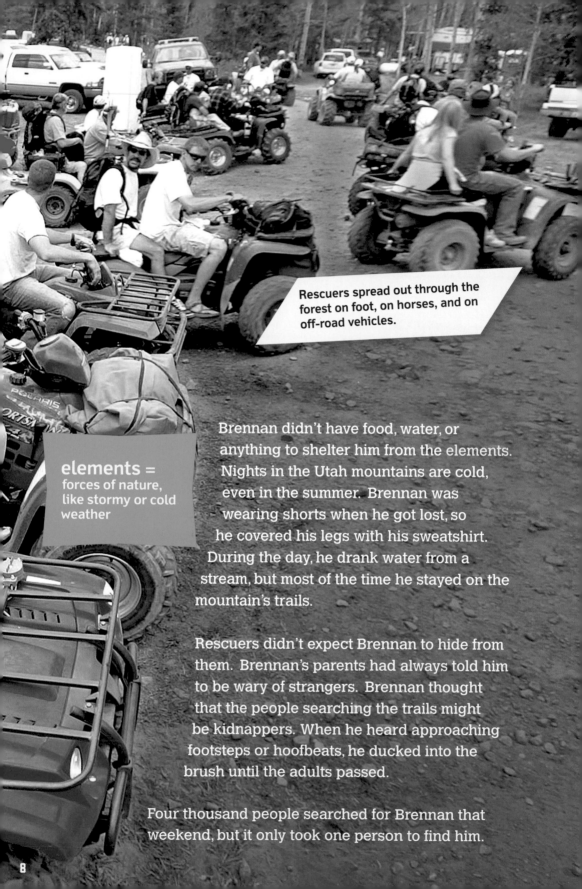

Rescuers spread out through the forest on foot, on horses, and on off-road vehicles.

elements = forces of nature, like stormy or cold weather

Brennan didn't have food, water, or anything to shelter him from the elements. Nights in the Utah mountains are cold, even in the summer. Brennan was wearing shorts when he got lost, so he covered his legs with his sweatshirt. During the day, he drank water from a stream, but most of the time he stayed on the mountain's trails.

Rescuers didn't expect Brennan to hide from them. Brennan's parents had always told him to be wary of strangers. Brennan thought that the people searching the trails might be kidnappers. When he heard approaching footsteps or hoofbeats, he ducked into the brush until the adults passed.

Four thousand people searched for Brennan that weekend, but it only took one person to find him.

Volunteer searcher Forrest Nunley joined the rescue effort on an off-road vehicle. He saw Brennan just as the boy emerged from behind a bush. Nunley identified himself and said he was there to help. He offered Brennan a peanut butter and jelly sandwich, some beef jerky, and licorice, all of which Brennan gobbled up. He had just survived four nights alone in the Uinta Mountains without food or clean water.

Brennan gave a news conference the day after his rescue, along with his mother (*left*) and sister (*right*).

9

THE LONE WOMAN OF SAN NICOLAS ISLAND

Imagine you are a member of a Native American group. You have been living on an island, but your friends and family are leaving for the mainland. A wild storm whirls around you as the last six members of your group board a rescue ship and sail away. You are left completely alone. How do you survive?

San Nicolas Island is 60 miles (97 km) off the coast of Southern California. It is part of a group of islands known as the Channel Islands. For eight thousand years, it was home to a Native American group called the Nicoleño. They lived in huts made of whalebone and stretched sealskin. They hunted sea mammals and fished in the surrounding waters to survive.

In 1811 Russian fur traders hired hunters to trap otters on San Nicolas. The hunters were only supposed to stay for a few weeks. They ended up living and fighting on the island until at least 1814.

Three hundred native people lived on the island when the hunters arrived. The Russians battled the Nicoleño. Most of the native men died. The group grew smaller. By 1835 only seven Nicoleño remained.

A group of priests from the mainland sent a ship to rescue the last seven Nicoleño. It was a stormy day in 1835. The rest of the details are not clear. Some stories say that one of the women went back to the village to rescue her baby. Others say that the baby fell overboard and the woman jumped in after her. But whatever the reason, the outcome was the same. As the storm grew worse, the rescuers accidentally left one woman behind.

After the storm departed, it started to become clear that the ship from the mainland would not be returning anytime soon.

For the next eighteen years, the Lone Woman of San Nicolas Island mastered the art of survival. Her early days alone were not easy. Men had always hunted, fished, and built shelters. She had to teach herself how to do these things. One of her biggest challenges was overcoming the idea that women couldn't do certain kinds of work.

She may have been the only human on San Nicolas, but the Lone Woman was far from alone. Animals of all shapes and sizes lived on the island, including birds, sea lions, and dogs. Living without human contact for a long time can be hard on one's mind. Historians think her companionship with animals helped keep her from going insane.

Though beautiful, California's Channel Islands are difficult places to survive.

In 1853 mainland authorities convinced a rancher from nearby Santa Barbara to search for the missing woman. The rancher and his men found the Lone Woman sitting near her hut skinning a seal. The woman, now around fifty years old, welcomed the men with a smile and a meal of roasted roots. The party stayed and hunted otters for three weeks. When it was time for them to leave, the Lone Woman gathered all of her possessions, including a rotting seal skull, and sailed with them to Santa Barbara.

Nobody on the mainland spoke her language, so the Lone Woman used hand signals to communicate. She seemed curious and happy and enjoyed all the new food, especially fresh fruit. But her happiness did not last long. The Lone Woman died of dysentery seven weeks after she arrived on the mainland. After eighteen years alone on a remote island, the last member of the Nicoleño group died weeks after joining other people on the mainland.

dysentery =
a disease leading
to severe diarrhea

Today San Nicolas Island is home to a US military base.

Lost in the South American Jungle

French hikers Loïc Pillois and Guilhem Nayral spent fifty-one days lost in the Amazon jungle. To survive, they ate seeds, insects, and giant spiders.

The two men had planned to hike through French Guiana to the little village of Saül in February 2007. It was a 60-mile (97 km) trip. The journey should have taken only eleven days. When they hadn't arrived at Saül by the twelfth day, they knew they were in trouble. The town is located in a valley, but all the nearby paths went uphill. They realized they must have made a wrong turn somewhere.

They decided the best thing to do was to stay in one place until searchers found them. They set up a camp. They were out of food, but they had a tarp, two hammocks, and a giant knife. The tarp became their roof.

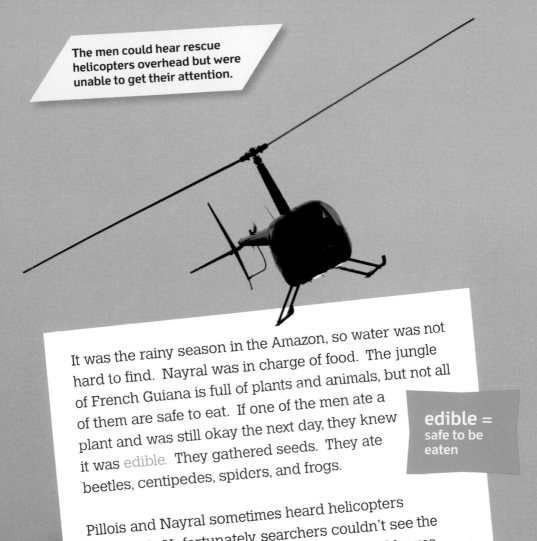

The men could hear rescue helicopters overhead but were unable to get their attention.

It was the rainy season in the Amazon, so water was not hard to find. Nayral was in charge of food. The jungle of French Guiana is full of plants and animals, but not all of them are safe to eat. If one of the men ate a plant and was still okay the next day, they knew it was edible. They gathered seeds. They ate beetles, centipedes, spiders, and frogs.

edible = safe to be eaten

Pillois and Nayral sometimes heard helicopters overhead. Unfortunately, searchers couldn't see the men through the thick layer of branches and leaves. After a few weeks, the helicopters stopped coming. The men knew the search had ended. They packed up their camp and started walking. Weak from hunger, they could only walk for about three hours each day.

Tarantulas may look frightening, but no species of tarantula has a bite that is actually fatal to humans.

The men were starving. Insects and seeds did not provide them with much energy. They eventually caught a 7-pound (3-kilogram) turtle after a week of hiking. They were so excited that they ate the entire thing, including the skin, scales, and claws. They heated the blood over a fire and drank it.

Nayral caught a mygale the next day. Mygales are a type of tarantula. He cooked the spider, but not long enough. Its sharp hairs made Nayral's tongue swell painfully. His lips went numb. He tried to keep hiking, but the pain was too great. He stayed behind while Pillois made one last attempt to find the village of Saül.

Pillois walked for a day and a half before he was spotted on Saül's airfield. Rescuers followed his directions, and Nayral was found four hours later. Pillois was in relatively good health, but Nayral was near death. Doctors said he would have died within three days if he hadn't been treated. "To have found Guilhem at this place is nothing short of a miracle," said a doctor. "That forest is as thick as broccoli."

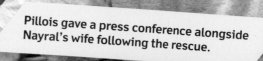

Pillois gave a press conference alongside Nayral's wife following the rescue.

Stranded in a Canyon

The rescue stretcher barely fit between the narrow canyon walls. Usually a rescuer would ride alongside as the stretcher was lifted up out of the canyon. But rescue workers had to get Ben Gowans to a hospital—and fast. The rescuer hopped off the stretcher, and Gowans was lifted up alone. The only way to go was up.

On April 17, 2002, Gowans and two friends descended into Leprechaun Canyon in Utah. This canyon is well known for being difficult to travel through. At places its walls are so close together that people get stuck. But Gowans was up for the challenge. He talked his friends into giving it a try.

descended = moved from a high area to a lower place

Gowans was not an experienced climber. He did not have a helmet or any other safety equipment. As he started to climb back out, fine, dry sand showered down. The edge of the canyon collapsed just as Gowans reached the top. He fell backward, bouncing between the walls until he hit the canyon floor 60 feet (18 meters) below. His head was bleeding inside, and his skull was fractured.

WHAT IS CANYONEERING?

Canyoneering is a sport that combines hiking, wading, and swimming in a canyon. Some people use the word to describe an easy hike. But serious canyoneers like more of a challenge. It can be dangerous, especially in places where the canyon walls are very close together. Ropes, helmets, and harnesses can help prevent injury.

Utah's beautiful landscapes can prove deadly when people do not possess the skills and equipment to survive them.

Without the skills to climb out, the three hikers were stuck. They spent a long, cold night at the bottom of the canyon. They did not know it at the time, but the cold was actually a good thing. It slowed the deadly swelling in Gowans's brain.

Twenty-five hours after the fall, the men spotted rescue helicopters overhead. They began shouting and banging their gear against the canyon wall. The rescuers spotted them, and they brought the men to safety. Gowans eventually made a full recovery. He does not remember the fall or the two weeks after his rescue. His experience has not kept him out of the wilderness. But now he wears a helmet when out on an adventure.

LOST IN LAVA

Gilbert Dewey Gaedcke figured he would be back before sunrise. It was April 2005, and the Texan was vacationing in Hawaii. He wanted to take a closer look at the Kilauea volcano on the island of Hawaii, also known as the Big Island. Volcanoes are best viewed at night, so Gaedcke waited until after dark to walk across the lava fields.

Lava fields do not make for easy hiking. In these areas, red-hot liquid rock that once flowed from the volcano cools into a hard, uneven surface. The jagged chunks of hardened lava can be as sharp as broken glass. Patches of junglelike plants grow on and through the rock, but there are no sources of drinking water.

It is easy to get lost in the dark lava fields. Gaedcke walked and walked, but he could not find his car again. When the sun rose, the air felt thick and hot. Even in the daylight, his car was nowhere to be found. He didn't have any food or water, and there was nothing he could use to make a shelter. However, Gaedcke did have his camera and its carrying case. And the case had a mirror. He tried reflecting sunlight off the mirror to signal helicopters overhead. Still nobody saw him. The sun was never in the right place

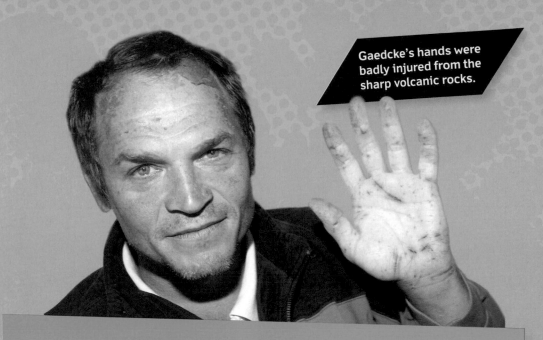

Gaedcke's hands were badly injured from the sharp volcanic rocks.

KILAUEA'S ERUPTIVE HISTORY

Kilauea is one of five volcanoes that make up the Big Island. It's the most active volcano on Earth. Kilauea has erupted sixty times since 1840. Lava has not stopped flowing from the volcano since January 1983. This chart shows the amount of lava released by eruptions between the 1820s and the 1980s.

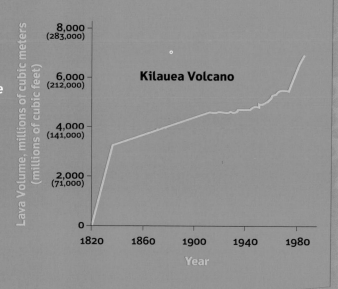

Kilauea Volcano

Lava Volume, millions of cubic meters (millions of cubic feet)

8,000 (283,000)
6,000 (212,000)
4,000 (141,000)
2,000 (71,000)
0

1820   1860   1900   1940   1980

Year

Gaedcke kept wandering through the lava fields for five days before a teenager aboard a tour helicopter finally spotted light flashing off his mirror. He was dehydrated and covered with cuts from the sharp rocks. But he had survived.

dehydrated= lost an unsafe amount of water or bodily fluid

Mushroom Hunters Go Missing

Dan and Belinda Conne and their twenty-five-year-old son Michael could not find their way out of the woods. The family had spent a warm day in January 2012 in Oregon hunting wild mushrooms. Now they were lost. They had no idea it would take six long, wet days to be rescued.

It rained the first night, so the Connes and their pet pit bull slept under a pile of branches and leaves. On the second day, they built a shelter, but it soon fell down. They finally huddled together in a large, leaky, hollow log.

A nearby creek provided water. But the family did not have food or warm clothes. The mushrooms they had collected could not be eaten raw. The Connes began getting desperate. They even talked about eating their dog. "I don't think we could have done it," Belinda later said. "I probably would have starved to death first."

hypothermia = a drop in body temperature to an unhealthy level

The Connes were only 200 yards (183 m) from the nearest group of searchers when a helicopter pilot finally spotted them. Dan was treated for back injuries. Belinda had hypothermia. And Michael had a sprained ankle and frostbite. All three were dehydrated.

And as for the mushrooms? Dan gave them away as soon as the family was rescued. "I don't ever want to see one of these again," he said.

The Conne family, including Dan, was grateful that their beloved dog survived the ordeal.

RESCUED BY MAN'S BEST FRIEND

Danelle Ballengee's hip bone was broken in four places. Three of the vertebrae in her back were cracked. She had lost a third of her blood. It was cold. Her dog was missing. The world-class adventure racer took a deep breath and wondered how she would survive.

Ballengee and her dog Taz had set out on a training run in the mountains of Moab, Utah, two days earlier on December 13, 2006. The temperature was cool. Ballengee wore light winter running gear. She had long underwear, pants, a shirt, a fleece jacket, and a hat. She carried a bottle of water and two energy gel packs.

She planned to run an 8-mile (13 km) loop off the beaten path. It would take ninety minutes. Her route included places where she needed to scramble up steep slopes. For an experienced adventure racer, that was part of the fun.

Ballengee was an hour into her run when her feet hit a patch of ice. She slipped, tumbling 40 feet (12 m) down the side of a slope and then another two stories straight to the ground. She landed on her feet, and then collapsed as pain shot through her body.

She couldn't stand. The main trail was 3 miles (5 km) away, and she would have to crawl. She managed to get on all fours, but her left leg wouldn't budge. She scooted her right knee forward, then reached back to pull her left knee forward. Crawl, pull, crawl, pull, over and over again. Five hours later, she had only gone a quarter of a mile (0.4 km).

Ballengee was an experienced racer. In 2000 she competed in a five-day race through China.

Her dog Taz appeared. He curled up next to her while she refilled her water bottle in a puddle. It was growing colder, so Ballengee did what she could to keep warm. She wiggled her fingers and toes and tapped her feet against the rocks.

Morning came. She tried crawling again. Pain spread through her legs and back worse than the day before. She screamed for ten hours, hoping that someone would be looking for her. But she hadn't told anybody where she was going. Who would realize she was in trouble?

Fortunately, her neighbor Dorothy Rossignol was nosy and proud of it. She noticed that Ballengee's truck was gone, but the lights in the house were on. When the lights were still on the next day, she called Ballengee's parents. They called the police.

As night began to fall over the snow-covered cliffs of Moab, Utah, there was no sign of help for Ballengee.

Thanks to Taz, rescuers finally found Ballengee at the bottom of an icy cliff.

When searchers found her car, they also found another clue: Taz. The reddish-brown dog was hungry and tired, but he wouldn't take the food they offered him. The searchers followed him back to the canyons.

After Taz disappeared over the top of a hill, rescuers followed his footprints. They found Taz lying next to Ballengee, resting his snout on her chest. She was alive. As Ballengee put it, "I wasn't ready to die."

10 Wilderness Survival Tips

1. Tell people where you're going and when you'll be back. People can't look for you if they don't know you're missing.

2. Bring extra clothing. It might be warm when you set out, but nights can get cold no matter where you are. Bring along a warm jacket and a hat in case you have to spend the night in the wild.

3. Pack more food and water than you think you'll need. It's easier to eat and drink what you already have than it is to find food or water in the wilderness. A good rule of thumb is to carry two quarts of water per person for an all-day hike.

4. Carry the right gear. Pack a pocketknife, a compass, a map, and matches or a lighter. Bring along a cell phone, but know that it might not work in all areas.

5. Go to where you can be seen. Stay on high, open ground so rescuers can easily spot you from land or air.

6. Yell "Help!" as loudly and often as you can. Carry a whistle to make calling for help easier.

7. Use signals. If you don't have matches or a lighter to build a fire, try using a mirror to reflect sunlight.

8. Find water. You can go a month without eating but only three days without water. If you can't find a stream or a lake, look for dew on plants and trees.

9. Build a shelter. It will protect you from rain, wind, and snow during the day and cold weather at night.

10. Don't panic. Stay calm and think clearly. Focus on one task at a time.

Dougherty, Joseph. *Miracle! Brennan Found Alive and Well*
http://www.deseretnews.com/article/print/600143277/Miracle-Brennan
-found-alive-and-well.html
Eleven-year-old Brennan Hawkins spent four nights alone in the Utah
mountains. Learn more about his experience in this news article written just
days after he was found.

Metzler, Brian. *Between a Dog and a Hard Place*
http://thebark.com/print/3110?page=show
Experts say that Taz, a three-year-old dog, was responsible for Danelle
Ballengee's rescue. Learn more about their friendship and how Taz helped
Danelle in her darkest moments.

Nayral, Guilhem. *Starving in the Amazon for Seven Weeks*
http://www.outsideonline.com/outdoor-adventure/outdoor-skills/survival
/Starving.html
Guilhem Nayral tells his story of survival in the Amazon jungle, including
what happened when he bit into that giant spider.

Robinson, Joe. *18 Years of Solitude: Marooned*
http://www.latimes.com/features/la-os-island15jun15,1,1046257.story
The story of the Lone Woman of San Nicolas Island sounds like a folktale.
Experts share the truth about the Lone Woman and how she was able to live
alone on an island for eighteen years.

Shimanski, Charley. *General Backcountry Safety*
http://www.mra.org/images/stories/training/backcountrysafety.pdf
Use this electronic guide to prepare for your outdoor adventure. Print it
out and bring it along so you know what to do in case of an emergency.

Stackpole Books. *Survival Wisdom & Know-How.* New York: Black Dog &
Leventhal, 2007.
Scouts, explorers, and nature lovers will find everything they need to
know in this volume of survival skills and knowledge. From tying knots to
identifying edible plants to building shelters, this big book covers all the
basics and then some.

Stroud, Les. *Will to Live: Dispatches from the Edge of Survival.*
New York: HarperCollins, 2011.
Survival expert Les Stroud takes you inside true tales of survival to show
what went wrong and what could have been done differently.

6   "Utah Boy's Ordeal Details Emerge," *CBS News*, February 11, 2009, http://www.cbsnews.com/8301-201_162-703669.html.

17   Henry Samuel, "Lost Trekkers Survive on Spider Diet," *Telegraph* (London), April 7, 2007, http://www.telegraph.co.uk/news/worldnews/1547928/Lost-trekkers-survive-on-spider-diet.html.

22   "Lost, Rescued Mushroom-Picking Family Considered Eating Pet Dog," *New York Daily News*, February 6, 2012, http://www.nydailynews.com/news/national/lost-rescued-mushroom-picking-family-considered-eating-pet-dog-article-1.1018276.

23   Ibid.

27   "Miracle in Moab: The Stunning Rescue of Danelle Ballengee," Summit Daily, December 22, 2006, http://www.summitdaily.com/article/20061222/NEWS/61222011.

INDEX

PHOTO ACKNOWLEDGMENTS

The images in this book are used with the permission of: © andreiuc88/Shutterstock Images, p. 4;
© Poliki/Shutterstock Images, p. 5; © Johnny Adolphson/Shutterstock Images, p. 6; © Douglas C.
Pizac/AP Images, pp. 7, 8; © Keith Johnson/Deseret Morning News/AP Images, p. 9; © Lemonan/
Shutterstock Images, p. 10; © David M. Schrader/Shutterstock Images, p. 11; © Rick Laverty/
Shutterstock Images, p. 12; NASA, p. 13; © Dr. Morley Read/Shutterstock Images, p. 14; © Trevor
Kelly/Shutterstock Images, p. 15; © worldwildlifewonders/Shutterstock Images, p. 16; © Jody
Amiet/AFP/Getty Images, p. 17; © Peter Wey/Shutterstock Images, p. 18; © AdStock RF/
Shutterstock Images, p. 19; © Marcel Clemens/Shutterstock Images, p. 20; © Tim Wright/AP
Images, p. 21; © Jeff McGraw/Shutterstock Images, p. 22; © TFoxFoto/Shutterstock Images, p. 23
(top); © Jeff Barnard/AP Images, p. 23 (bottom); © Nina B/Shutterstock Images, pp. 24, 27; © AP
Images, p. 25; © Charles L. Bolin/Shutterstock Images, p. 26; © Blend Images/Shutterstock
Images, p. 28; © ChameleonsEye/Shutterstock Images, p. 29.

Front cover: Petty Officer Shawn Eggert/U.S. Coast Guard

Main body text set in Calvert MT Std Regular 11/16.
Typeface provided by Monotype Typography.